Murphy's New Home

Never Underestimate the Power of Love

Lived by Darlene C. Nickerson
Written by Stacey E. Hathaway
Illustrated by Maureen Tracy Patrolia

Based on a True Story

I dedicate this book to my mother Marjorie "Tillie" Soule Nickerson, for she encouraged my love of horses so many, many years ago.

To Copper, my first horse in need. I had six wonderful years with you, my friend. I miss you every day.

To my family and friends for their unending support and patience.

To the writer, Stacey; and illustrator, Maureen, for donating so much of their time and love on this book to help this rescue survive.

Special thanks to Dr. Costa, Murphy's doctor at Tufts.

ISBN: 978-0-615-42273-2

This book was printed in the United States of America.

Hi! My name is Murphy. I am a four-year-old horse, and Shire is my breed. Shires are large work horses originally bred in England. We have enormous feet that help us pull heavy carts and wagons.

I'm very excited because today I go to my new home!

I am also getting a new mommy and a bunch of new
brothers and sisters.

My new home is called Black Feather Horse Rescue,
and my new mom is going to take extra special care of me.

You see, I'm sick. I have trouble swallowing so I am fed through a tube. My new mom is going to do all that she can to help me feel better. I am very nervous about meeting everyone and learning my way around my new home.

Here I am.   It was a long trip, but I've finally arrived at the Black Feather barn.

My new room is called a stall and it's just perfect. It's so big I can lie down if I want to. Looking out the top of the door I can see my new brothers and sisters horsing around in the yard. I can't wait until I am feeling well enough to join them.

Oh, look! A pond and stream filled with lots of fish. There's "Billy" the goat and all his friends. I see chickens scratching in the dirt and a playful dog. Is that a pasture on the hill? There is so much to see that I can't wait to explore the farm.

Across from my stall are two other horses that live here at the rescue. Luke, my new older brother, has assured me that I'll be hugged and kissed every day and that Mom will do her very best to make me healthy.

Thunder Moon, my new younger brother, has offered to be my friend and show me around. He says that we'll have lots of fun together and he's even challenged me to a trot around the paddock when I'm feeling better.

Here comes Mom with my dinner. I'm fed through a tube in my neck. No, it doesn't hurt a bit. It's not what I'm used to, and boy do I miss eating hay and grass, but it sure fills up my belly. With mom so close when she feeds me, I get to sniff how good she smells, and she's always telling me how special and loved I am. That feels really nice!

After Mom feeds me, she gives me my water. In my stall, my water bags hang above my head. Mom fills them with fresh, clean water and connects them to the tube in my neck. She does this three times a day to make sure I get enough to drink.

Did you know that horses can drink 10 or more gallons of water a day?

Not being able to swallow has its downfalls.
One of them is that I always have a runny nose.
Thank goodness it doesn't stop Mom from kissing me.
Once I even sneezed on her friend. What a mess!
I was so embarrassed.

Another downfall is that I can’t eat any hay.
I’m not outside in the paddock with the other horses
because they would share their hay pile with me.
Mom is afraid I might choke. She tries to spend a lot
of time with me, but the rest of my family needs her too.
I sometimes find myself alone in the barn.
As much as I love my stall, it can get very boring!

I look forward to the walks Mom and I take every day. We walk along the wooded paths around the barn while the birds sing and the squirrels rustle in the bushes. Just standing in the sun with my eyes closed is wonderful. The pine trees are humongous! I can't wait until I can swallow again so I'll be able to breathe in their scent.

Mom puts me to bed just before dark. My stall is filled with warm, soft shavings for me to snuggle in. This is my most favorite time because I am surrounded by my brothers and sisters for the night. I am so blessed. I love my new home!

Nine whole months later........

Hi everyone! It's me Murphy. I've settled in just fine at my new home. I love everyone and they love me. I feel like a king. Best of all, I can now swallow and eat meals on my own. Yippee – I can eat hay! I still need to drink my water through a tube, but I'm feeling great! It took a long time and a lot of hard work to get to where I am today, but I just know I'll be back to my old self any day now!

This is not "the end" for this is truly the *beginning*, not only for Murphy, but for our collection of stories from the Black Feather Rescue Barn. Please stay tuned for more books in this series.

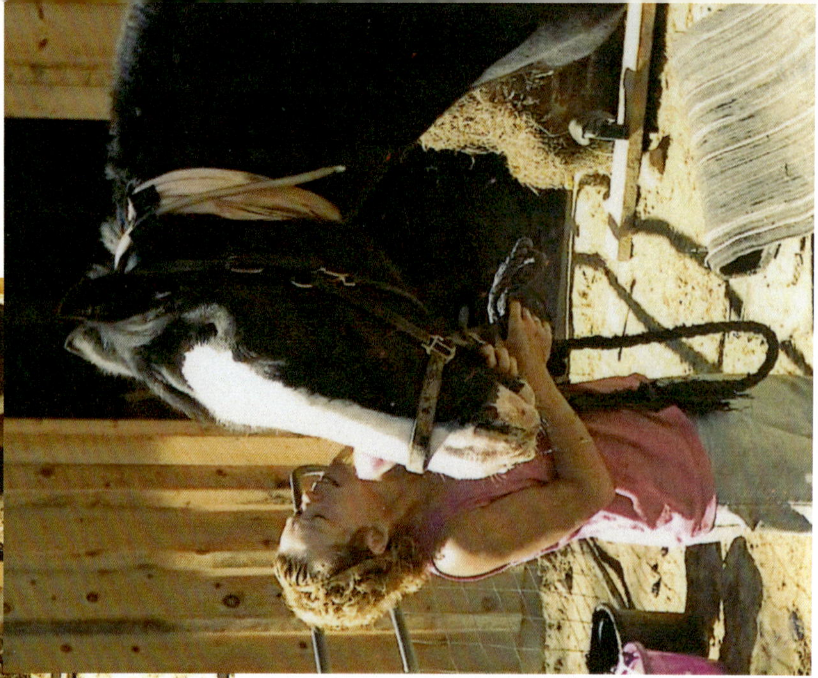

At the age of three, Murphy's Law contracted an infection in his guttural pouch. Most horses do not survive this type of infection. Those that do, usually suffer a numbing of the throat, leaving them unable to swallow. At the time that Murphy was surrendered to the rescue, his prognosis was poor. Although Darlene Nickerson had to tube-feed and water him five to six times a day, often in the middle of the night and in harsh weather, she never gave up hope or entertained the thought that he might not ever eat on his own again. Nine months after arriving at the rescue, having survived pneumonia, Murphy began to slowly swallow on his own. It has been a gradual process but Murphy now eats 100% of his food on his own. He has begun to put back on the weight that he lost and is looking fantastic. He still receives his water intravenously through the tube in his neck several times a day, but everyone hopes it is only a matter of time before he drinks on his own as well. Throughout his whole ordeal, Murphy has remained a loving, peaceful and dignified horse... never once acting out against his circumstances. A perfect gentleman!

Recently, it was learned that the majority of horses that survive this type of infection never swallow again. He is definitely Black Feather's miracle. Rather than "Murphy's Law," he is affectionately referred to as just plain old Murphy now.

BLACK FEATHER

HORSE RESCUE

would like to personally thank the following sponsors:

Oak Paws Pet Club

Chiltonville Fly Fishing Club

Gilbert Trout Hatchery

Morrison's Farm & Garden

The Medas Family of Norton

Powder Horn Press, Inc.